SUPER-QUICK
MUFFIN TIN
MEALS

70 Recipes *for* Perfectly Portioned Comfort Food in a Cup

Melanie LaDue

Race Point
PUBLISHING
www.racepointpub.com
New York, NY

Race Point Publishing
An imprint of Quarto Publishing Group USA Inc.
142 West 36th Street, 4th Floor
New York, NY 10018

RACE POINT PUBLISHING and the distinctive Race Point Publishing logo are trademarks of Quarto Publishing Group USA, Inc.

Created by Warren Street Books
Design: CThompsonDesigns, NYC

Text and photography © 2015 by Melanie LaDue

Photos used under license from Shutterstock appear on pages 8, 12, 20, 147.

ISBN: 978-1-63106-159-2

The recipe for Cheeseburger Pies on page 49 has been reprinted here with the permission of Leigh Anne Wilkes at www.yourhomebasedmom.com.

Library of Congress Cataloging-in-Publication data is available

Printed in China

10 9 8 7 6 5 4 3 2 1

www.racepointpub.com

When I became a new mom, I had visions of creating perfect home-cooked meals every night and freshly baked muffins every morning. Then, reality set in, and all too often I found myself stopping for fast food on my way home from work. Mealtime, for us, needs to be fast and easy, but delicious (of course).

I'm all about easy food. I just don't have time to come up with meal ideas that can be prepared and eaten quickly, and a girl can only come up with so many crock pot meals. My daughter loves to work with me in the kitchen, which is what gave me a blog post idea for food that can be cooked in a muffin tin with Crescent Rolls—things she could help me make. As I searched online, I found so many recipes that were NOT MUFFINS that could be made in a muffin tin, and the roundup for my site, Reasons To Skip The Housework, came together in a matter of 20 minutes. The response I got from blog readers about the fabulous recipes they were trying from this one blog post was huge! I knew I was on to something.

So many moms can tell you, it's just easier to have everything pre-portioned out and simple to grab and go. You don't have to be hosting a party to want small, bite-size food you can eat and walk and occasionally drive with!

I don't have time to make homemade mashed potatoes or homemade chili or marinara sauce. Luckily, there are many store-bought brands that do a great job with these. Most of my muffin tin recipes use Crescent Rolls or Crescent

Roll Dough Sheets, and many use refrigerated pizza dough and biscuits, too. These all can be found in the refrigerated section, next to the cheese or cookie dough, my other favorite go-to ingredients. I buy in bulk and always have them on hand for a quick, last-minute muffin tin meal.

You don't have to own dozens of fancy pans and utensils to make muffin tin meals, either. You'll need a knife or a small metal spatula, since everything has to be "popped" out of the tins. You will need a cooling rack and one regular size muffin tin and one mini muffin tin, but that's pretty much it. These are simple recipes, using simple ingredients, for simple meal times!

Melanie LaDue

BREAKFAST

I don't particularly want to be a morning person. But with a job, husband, child, and pretty much everything in real life after college, I really don't have much choice. These muffin tin breakfasts are easy, fast, can often be made ahead of time, and will get your day off to a good start without having to commit to a sit-down meal. They're also perfectly fine for the rare day when there is nothing on the calendar and mom and daughter just possibly might stay in their jammies until noon.

GRANOLA BITES

MAKES 24 mini granola bites

PREP TIME: 20 minutes

1 banana (an overly ripe banana is
   easiest to mash)
2 cups (470g) oatmeal
¼ cup (60g) applesauce
2 tablespoons (40g) honey
½ teaspoon (2.1g) vanilla
½ teaspoon (1.15g) cinnamon
⅛ teaspoon (.3g) nutmeg
⅛ teaspoon (.3g) ginger
Yogurt of choice, for serving
Berries of choice, for serving
   (optional)

Preheat oven to 350°F (180°C). Spray
24 mini muffin cups with cooking spray.

Put banana in a medium bowl and mash
well. Add remaining ingredients to
the bowl and stir to blend well. Press
1 tablespoon (15g) of mixture into
each mini muffin cup. Bake for 20–25
minutes, until a toothpick comes
out clean.

Using a knife or a mini metal spatula,
transfer the bites from the cups to a
rack to cool. To serve, top with a dab of
yogurt and a berry, if desired.

TIP:
Add a variety of
fruits and nuts to the
granola mixture to
make your own
variations!

BAKED EGGS

MAKES 12 whole eggs

PREP TIME: 3 minutes

12 eggs in their shells

Preheat oven to 325°F (170°C) and prepare a cold water bath.

Place 1 egg in each of 12 regular size muffin cups. Bake eggs for 30 minutes.

Wearing oven mitts, remove eggs, one at a time, from the muffin cups and transfer to the cold water bath. Let eggs cool in the water for 10 minutes. Peel and eat!

BAKED EGGS WITH HERBS

MAKES 12 eggs

PREP TIME: 5 minutes

12 eggs
Salt, to taste
Freshly ground black pepper, to taste
1 teaspoon (1.3g) fresh basil, chopped
1 teaspoon (1.3g) fresh thyme,
    chopped

TIP:
Serve the eggs on an English muffin topped with American cheese, or serve with bacon and fruit for the perfect breakfast! Dried herbs are a great option when you don't have fresh herbs.

Heat oven to 350°F (180°C). Spray 12 regular size muffin cups with cooking spray.

Crack the eggs, one at a time, dropping each into a muffin cup and discarding shells. Sprinkle the eggs with salt, pepper, and herbs. Bake for 15–20 minutes, until eggs are cooked through.

Transfer the tin to a rack and allow the eggs to cool slightly. Using a knife or a mini metal spatula, carefully pry the eggs out of the tin and transfer to plates.

CHEESY SAUSAGE SCRAMBLED EGGS

MAKES 10 egg cups

PREP TIME: 15 minutes

10 large eggs
1 cup (110g) cooked ground sausage
1 cup (120g) shredded cheese, such as
  cheddar, Colby Jack, or mozzarella
Freshly ground black pepper, to taste

TIP:
Add finely chopped spinach, bell peppers, and mushrooms to the egg mixture for a heartier egg muffin!

Preheat oven to 350°F (180°C). Spray 10 regular size muffin cups with cooking spray.

Crack the eggs into a medium bowl, add 1 tablespoon (15ml) of water, and scramble with a fork until well mixed. Fill muffin cups half full with egg mixture. Top egg mixture with sausage and cheese, dividing it equally among cups, and season with pepper. Bake 20–25 minutes, until eggs are cooked through. (When eggs bounce back to the touch, they're ready!)

Using a knife or a mini metal spatula, lift eggs out of tin and transfer to plates. Serve immediately.

HASH BROWN CUPS

MAKES 12 servings

PREP TIME: 10 minutes

1 (20-ounce, 560-g) bag shredded
  hash browns
2 green onions, chopped
¼ cup (20g) Parmesan cheese
1 teaspoon (6g) salt
Freshly ground black pepper, to taste
2 tablespoons (28g) olive oil

Preheat oven to 350°F (180°C). Spray 12 regular size muffin cups with cooking spray.

Combine potatoes, green onions, cheese, salt, and pepper in a medium bowl. Add olive oil and toss with a fork. Spoon mixture into muffin cups, filling cups, then press down to pack mixture. Bake for 60 minutes, or until hash browns are browned and crispy.

Transfer tin to a rack and let hash brown cups cool 5 minutes. Using a knife or mini metal spatula, lift hash browns out of tin and transfer to plates.

TIP:
For cheesier hash browns, add cheddar cheese to the potato mixture. You can also fill the tins with the potato mixture the night before and store, covered, in the fridge.

HASH BROWN EGG NESTS

MAKES 12 servings

PREP TIME: 15 minutes

2 cups (220g) shredded hash browns
½ cup (60g) cheddar cheese, shredded
¼ cup (40g) green onions, chopped
3 strips cooked bacon, cut into pieces
(optional)
½ teaspoon (3g) seasoned salt
Freshly ground black pepper, to taste
Dried Italian seasoning
12 eggs

TIP:
Take eggs out of oven 5 minutes before they are cooked and sprinkle additional cheese, to taste, on top. Return to oven and bake until cheese is melted.

Preheat oven to 400°F (200°C). Spray 12 regular size muffin cups with cooking spray.

Combine potatoes, cheese, green onions, bacon (if using), salt, pepper, and Italian seasoning in a medium bowl. Divide mixture among the muffin cups, then press down firmly to pack mixture. Crack one egg into each cup and add more pepper. Bake for 35–40 minutes, until eggs are cooked, depending on how firm you like your eggs!

Transfer tin to a rack and let nests cool 5 minutes. Using a knife or mini metal spatula, lift egg nests out of tin and transfer to plates.

HASH BROWN TOMATO EGG FRITTATAS

MAKES 12 servings

PREP TIME: 15 minutes

2 cups (220g) shredded hash browns
1 cup (115g) cheddar cheese
1 cup (150g) cherry tomatoes
8 eggs

Preheat oven to 350°F (180°C). Spray 12 regular size muffin cups with cooking spray.

Combine potatoes, cheese, and tomatoes in a medium bowl. Beat eggs in a separate bowl and pour into potato mixture, stirring to combine. Divide mixture among cups. Bake for 15 minutes, or until eggs are cooked through.

Transfer tin to a rack and let frittatas cool 5 minutes. Using a knife or mini metal spatula, lift frittatas out of tin and transfer to plates.

TIP:
Add cooked, chopped sausage to the mixture before baking for meaty breakfast frittatas.

TIP:
Use almond milk in place of 2% milk for a dairy-free option.

OATMEAL CUPS

MAKES 12 oatmeal cups

PREP TIME: 15 minutes

1 ½ cups (355ml) milk
2 ½ cups (200g) old-fashioned
   rolled oats
2 bananas, peeled and sliced
3 teaspoons (6.9g) cinnamon, or
   to taste
¼ teaspoon (1.5g) salt
2 ½ teaspoons (12ml) vanilla extract
Suggested toppings: dried cranberries,
   fresh berries, chopped nuts, raisins

Spray 12 regular size muffin cups with cooking spray.

Bring 2 ½ cups (570ml) water and the milk to a boil in a medium pot. Sprinkle in oats and reduce heat to a constant simmer. Add bananas, cinnamon, and salt and stir to combine. Cook 8–10 minutes, stirring occasionally and adding more milk or water if mixture becomes dry. (Mixture will thicken as it cools.) Remove pot from the heat and add vanilla extract. Spoon mixture into muffin cups, dividing it evenly. Add desired toppings and press lightly into the oatmeal.

Transfer tin to a rack and let oatmeal cups cool for 20–30 minutes. Transfer tin to the freezer and freeze cups 4–5 hours. Using a knife or mini metal spatula, transfer oatmeal cups to a freezer bag and store in freezer for up to 3 months.

To reheat in microwave: Thaw as many muffin cups as you'll need in the fridge overnight in a microwave-safe bowl or a mason jar. When ready to serve, place bowl or jar in the microwave with a splash of milk and heat in 30 second intervals, stirring after each, until hot. Add milk as needed.

PUFFY PANCAKES

MAKES 12 pancakes

PREP TIME: 15 minutes

1 cup (235ml) milk
1 cup (158g) flour
6 eggs
¼ cup (56g) melted butter
Dash of salt
1 teaspoon (4.8ml) vanilla extract

TIP:
Sprinkle the pancakes with powdered sugar or drizzle with honey for a special treat.

Heat oven to 400°F (200°C). Spray 12 regular size muffin cups with cooking spray (spray generously or the pancakes will stick).

Combine all ingredients in a medium bowl and blend with a hand-held electric mixer on high for 3 minutes. Pour mixture into muffin cups, filling them half full. Bake pancakes 15 minutes, or until nice and puffy.

Transfer tins to a rack and let pancakes cool for 3–5 minutes. Using a knife or mini metal spatula, carefully remove the pancakes from the cups and transfer to plates. The pancakes will drop in the center as they cool, and that's perfect! Serve the pancakes, drizzled with syrup, and add your favorite fruit.

PESTO EGG MINI QUICHES

MAKES 12 servings

PREP TIME: 15 minutes

3 ounces (85g) cream cheese, softened
⅓ cup (71ml) milk
1 tablespoon (17g) store-bought
   basil pesto
½ teaspoon (3g) salt
¼ teaspoon (.5g) freshly ground
   black pepper
3 large eggs
1 frozen pie crust (homemade or
   store-bought), thawed slightly
1 tablespoon (4g) chopped fresh basil

Preheat oven to 350°F (180°C). Spray 12 regular size muffin cups with cooking spray.

Combine cream cheese, milk, pesto, salt, and pepper in a bowl and mix well. Add eggs and blend well. Using a 3-inch-wide (7.5-cm-wide) glass, cut out 12 circles of pie crust. Place a pie crust circle into each muffin cup and press down, keeping the pie crust pressed against the sides. Spoon egg mixture into pie crusts, filling each half full. Bake quiches for 20–25 minutes, until cooked through. (Use a toothpick to check for doneness.)

Transfer tin to a rack and let quiches cool 3–5 minutes. Using a knife or mini metal spatula, carefully remove the quiches from the cups and transfer to plates. Top each quiche with chopped basil and serve immediately.

CHERRY CHEESE DANISH BITES

MAKES 32 bites

PREP TIME: 20 minutes

2 (8-ounce, 225-g) packages frozen pastry dough sheets, thawed

1 (8-ounce, 225-g) package cream cheese, softened

¾ cup (90g) powdered sugar (divided)

1 small egg white

1 (14-ounce, 392-g) can cherry pie filling

1 ½ tablespoons (25ml) milk

½ teaspoon (2.4ml) vanilla extract

TIP:
Use apple pie filling or blueberry pie filling for different variations of this delicious breakfast!

Preheat oven to 350°F (180°C). Spray 32 mini muffin cups with cooking spray.

Cut each thawed pastry sheet into 16 equal squares. Place one square into each muffin cup. Mix cream cheese, half of the powdered sugar, and the egg white in a medium bowl until well blended. Spoon 1 tablespoon (15g) of mixture into each muffin cup. Top with a small spoonful of cherry pie filling (make sure there's one cherry in each spoonful!). Bake for 25 minutes.

Meanwhile, make the icing: mix remaining powdered sugar, milk, and vanilla extract in a bowl and set aside.

When the Danish bites are cooked, transfer the tins to a rack and allow the bites to cool for 5 minutes. Using a knife or mini metal spatula, remove the bites from the cups. Drizzle icing on bites and serve immediately.

MAIN DISHES

When I got married my mom gave me a recipe box filled with details on how to spend afternoons preparing family favorites for the many meals in my future. Nice. But reality is, I don't always have time to make full meals. Give these little main dish gems a try and you'll have some new favorites that are fast to fix and nearly impossible to mess up. Occasionally, if you're also short on time to eat, you can even pop a couple onto a napkin and rush out the door.

TIP:
Change up the veggies by adding cooked or thawed frozen asparagus, broccoli, or cauliflower pieces to the mixture!

CHICKEN POT PIES

MAKES 12 pot pies

PREP TIME: 15 minutes

2 (8-ounce, 225-g) refrigerated
  packages Crescent Recipe Creations
  (Seamless Dough Sheet)
1 (10 ¾-ounce, 301-g) can condensed
  cream of chicken soup
½ cup (120ml) milk
2 cups (220g) cooked chicken, cubed
1 (12-ounce, 340-g) package frozen
  mixed vegetables (carrots, green
  beans, corn, peas), thawed
1 cup (115g) shredded cheddar cheese

Preheat oven to 375°F (190°C).
Spray 12 regular size muffin cups
with cooking spray.

Unroll crescent roll sheets. Using a
3-inch-wide (7.5-cm-wide) glass, cut out
12 circles from the dough and fit one
circle into each muffin cup. Stir together
the soup, milk, chicken, and vegetables
in a medium bowl and spoon the
mixture into the muffin cups, dividing
it evenly. Sprinkle the tops with
cheese. Bake for 20–25 minutes, until
the crust is golden brown.

Using a knife or a mini metal spatula,
transfer the pot pies from the cups to
plates and serve immediately.

MEATLOAF CUPS

MAKES 10 meatloaf cups

PREP TIME: 10 minutes

1 pound (455g) ground beef
1 egg
½ cup (120ml) milk
¾ cup (81g) bread crumbs
½ teaspoon (3g) garlic salt
½ teaspoon (1g) freshly ground
   black pepper
Ketchup, for serving

Preheat oven to 350°F (180°C). Spray 10 regular size muffin cups with cooking spray. Mix together all ingredients, except ketchup, in a bowl until well blended. Divide mixture among cups, pressing down gently to pack. Bake for 20–25 minutes.

Remove tin from the oven and, using a knife or mini metal spatula, lift the meatloaf from the muffin cups and transfer to plates. Top each with ketchup (or serve ketchup on the side) and serve immediately.

TIP:
Top the baked meatloaf cups with whipped mashed potatoes and bake for 5 more minutes to brown the tips, then add chives before serving!

LASAGNA CUPS

MAKES 12 servings

PREP TIME: 15 minutes

1 (9-ounce, 252-g) box lasagna noodles (you'll need at least 12 noodles)
1 (15-ounce, 427-g) tub ricotta cheese
1 egg, whisked
2 teaspoons (3g) Italian seasoning
½ cup (75g) mozzarella cheese
2 cups (470ml) bottled marinara sauce

TIP:
Add crumbled cooked Italian sausage to the marinara sauce for a meaty version!

Preheat oven to 375°F (190°C). Spray 12 regular size muffin cups with cooking spray.

Cook the lasagna noodles according to package instructions. Drain and cut into 2-inch (5-cm) pieces. Combine the ricotta cheese, egg, and herbs in a medium bowl.

Layer lasagna noodles in the muffin cups with ricotta cheese mixture, mozzarella, and marinara sauce, ending with a sprinkle of mozzarella cheese on the top layer. (Noodles will curl a tad as you layer. Push down the edges as you fill and layer.) Bake for 25–30 minutes, until cheese is bubbling and golden brown.

Remove tin from oven and, using a knife or mini metal spatula, transfer the lasagna from the cups to plates and serve immediately.

MEATBALL SUBS

MAKES 8 subs

PREP TIME: 15 minutes

1 (8-ounce, 225-g) refrigerated
   package Crescent Original
   (8 Dinner Rolls)
10-12 packaged pre-cooked meatballs
1 cup (235ml) bottled marinara sauce
1 ½ cups (225g) shredded mozzarella
   cheese
Dried Italian seasonings, to taste

TIP:
Serve with
additional warm
marinara sauce
for dipping.

Preheat oven to 375°F (190°C). Spray 8 regular size muffin cups with cooking spray.

Unroll crescent rolls and separate along perforation marks. Cut meatballs into quarters and put 1 or 2 pieces (depending on size of meatballs) in center of each crescent roll. Top meatballs with a small spoonful of marinara sauce, a sprinkle of cheese, and a dash of Italian seasoning. Wrap crescent roll around meatball, fold edges over, and pinch closed. Place each sub in a muffin cup. Bake for 18–20 minutes, until rolls are golden brown.

Remove tin from oven and, using a knife or mini metal spatula, transfer the meatball subs to plates. Serve warm.

CHICKEN ENCHILADA POCKETS

MAKES 8 pockets

PREP TIME: 15 minutes

1 (8-ounce, 225-g) refrigerated package Crescent Original (8 Dinner Rolls)

3 ounces (85g) cream cheese

½ cup (58g) cheddar cheese

1 cup (110g) finely chopped cooked chicken

⅔ cup (235ml) red enchilada sauce

¼ cup (15g) fresh cilantro leaves, chopped

TIP:
Sprinkle with additional shredded cheddar cheese with a few minutes left to bake.

Preheat oven to 375°F (190°C). Spray 8 regular size muffin cups with cooking spray.

Unroll crescent rolls and separate along perforation marks. Mix together cream cheese, cheddar cheese, chicken, and enchilada sauce in a medium bowl. Put a small spoonful of the mixture on the center of each roll and sprinkle with cilantro. Pull the corners of the crescent roll to the center of the mixture, then bring the tiny end of the crescent roll up and over, forming a closed roll. Pinch together the edges and place in the muffin cups. Bake for 12–15 minutes, until the pockets are golden brown.

Remove tin from oven and, using a knife or mini metal spatula, transfer the pockets to plates. Before serving, drizzle additional enchilada sauce on top of the pockets and top with sour cream. Serve immediately.

TIP:
Skip the meatballs and add cooked Italian sausage to the center of the spaghetti nest.

SPAGHETTI NESTS

MAKES 12 spaghetti nests

PREP TIME: 15 minutes

8 ounces (225g) spaghetti noodles

3 egg whites

1 ½ cups (335ml) bottled marinara
  sauce

1 cup (115g) mozzarella cheese,
  shredded

12 packaged pre-cooked meatballs

1 tablespoon (2.5g) chopped fresh
  basil

Preheat oven to 400°F (200°C) . Spray 12 regular size muffin cups with cooking spray. Cook spaghetti according to package directions.

Place egg whites into a medium bowl and whisk. Add cooked spaghetti, marinara sauce, and ¾ cup (84g) mozzarella cheese and mix well.

Using tongs, transfer spaghetti mixture into muffin cups, pressing up the sides to make little nests. Bake for 12 minutes, or until the nests are melted and bubbly.

While the nests are baking, heat the meatballs according to package directions.

Place one meatball in each baked nest and sprinkle nests with the remaining mozzarella cheese. Return nests to the oven and bake for 3–5 minutes more to melt the cheese.

Remove tin from oven and, using a knife or mini metal spatula, transfer the nests to plates. Sprinkle with basil and serve immediately.

MINI CHICKEN TACOS

MAKES 24 mini tacos

PREP TIME: 15 minutes

1 tablespoon (15ml) olive oil, plus
   additional for brushing
   wonton wrappers
2–3 cups (220g-330g) cooked chicken,
   finely chopped or shredded
½ small red bell pepper, finely chopped
½ small green bell pepper, finely
   chopped
1 teaspoon (1.5g) taco seasoning
24 wonton wrappers
1 cup (115g) cheddar cheese, shredded
Optional toppings: sour cream,
   diced tomatoes, cilantro, onion,
   chopped lettuce

Preheat oven to 375°F (190°C). Spray
24 mini muffin cups with cooking spray.

Heat olive oil in a skillet over moderate
heat until hot but not smoking. Add
chicken and bell peppers and cook,
stirring, until cooked through. Add taco
seasoning and mix well. Remove skillet
from heat and set aside.

Working with one wonton wrapper at
a time, place wonton on a flat surface
and spray or brush with olive oil making
sure to cover the tips, then fit wonton
into a mini muffin cup. Continue until
all wrappers are oiled and fitted into
cups. Bake wonton cups in oven for 5–8
minutes, until edges are nice and golden.

Fill wonton cups with reserved
chicken mixture and sprinkle tops
with shredded cheese. Bake tacos 3–5
minutes, until cheese is melted.

Remove tin from oven and, using a knife
or mini metal spatula, transfer tacos to
plates. Serve immediately with desired
toppings.

TIP:
Make in a full size muffin tin for larger tacos and layer with refried beans for a more filling meal.

CHEESEBURGER PIES

MAKES 12 burger pies

PREP TIME: 20 minutes

1 tablespoon (15ml) olive oil
1 pound (455g) lean ground beef
    (at least 80%)
1 large onion, chopped (1 cup, 160g)
1 cup (115g) shredded cheddar cheese
    (4 ounces)
1 tablespoon (15ml) Worcestershire
    sauce
1 teaspoon (1.5g) garlic salt
½ cup (61g) Original Bisquick™ mix
½ cup (120ml) milk
2 eggs
12 mini kosher dill pickles,
    for serving (optional)
Ketchup and mustard, for serving

Preheat oven to 375°F (190°C).
Spray 12 regular size muffin cups with
cooking spray.

Heat oil in a 10-inch (25.4-cm) skillet over medium-high heat until hot but not smoking. Add beef and onion and cook, stirring occasionally, for 5–7 minutes, until meat is cooked through. Add cheese, Worcestershire sauce, and garlic salt and stir to combine. Remove skillet from heat and set aside.

In a medium bowl, whisk together Bisquick, milk, and eggs until blended. Spoon a scant tablespoon (15g) of Bisquick mixture into each muffin cup. Top with about ¼ cup (55g) burger mixture, then spoon another scant tablespoon (15g) Bisquick mixture on top. Bake about 30 minutes, or until toothpick inserted in center comes out clean and muffin tops are golden brown.

Transfer tin to a rack and let pies cool for 5 minutes. With thin knife, loosen sides of muffins from cups and transfer, top sides up, to a serving plate. Serve with garnishes, if desired.

PUFF PASTRY CHICKEN SALAD

MAKES 10 salad cups

PREP TIME: 20 minutes

1 box frozen puff pastry sheets
   (2 sheets), thawed
1 cup (110g) cooked chicken, diced
1 tablespoon (10g) red onion, diced
1 tablespoon (7.5g) celery, diced
2 teaspoons (10ml) lemon juice
2 teaspoons (10g) mayonnaise
¼ teaspoon (1.25ml) Dijon mustard
Dash of hot sauce
Salt and freshly ground black pepper,
   to taste
Fresh basil or parsley, for garnish

TIP:
Add lemon pepper
for extra zest!

Set pastry sheets on counter to thaw. Preheat oven to 350°F (180°C). Spray 10 regular size muffin cups with cooking spray.

Cut puff pastry into 2- to 3-inch (5- to 7.5cm) squares and fit each square into a muffin cup. Bake for 7–9 minutes, or until lightly golden.

While pastry bakes: put remaining ingredients, except fresh basil or parsley garnish, into a bowl and stir to combine.

Remove tin from oven and transfer to a rack to let puff pastry cups cool. When cups are cool, scoop a small amount of chicken salad into each cup. With a knife or mini metal spatula lift cups out of tin and transfer to plates. Garnish with fresh basil or parsley.

CHILI CORNBREAD CUPS

MAKES 12 chili cups

PREP TIME: 10 minutes

1 (16-ounce, 455-g) box cornbread mix

2 cups (512g) cooked or store-bought chili

Optional topping: 1 ½ cups (173g cheddar cheese, shredded)

Preheat oven to 350°F (180°C). Spray 12 regular size muffin cups with cooking spray.

Mix cornbread as directed on box and fill muffin cups two-thirds full with cornbread mixture. Bake for 10–12 minutes, until a toothpick comes out clean.

Reheat chili while cornbread bakes. As soon as the muffins come out of the oven, use bottom of a shot glass or other small glass to push down center of muffins. Spoon hot chili into cornbread cups, almost filling them, and sprinkle tops with cheese, if desired. Using a knife or mini metal spatula transfer chili cups to plates and serve hot.

TIP:
Use a mixture of yellow and white cheddars for varied flavor and color.

CHILI DOG ROLLS

MAKES 12 chili dogs

PREP TIME: 15 minutes

2 (8-ounce, 255-g) refrigerated
packages Crescent Original
(8 Dinner Rolls)
3 hot dogs
2 cups (512g) cooked or store-bought
chili
1–2 cups (115g - 230g) cheddar cheese,
shredded
Ketchup or extra chili, for dipping

TIP:
Add chopped
onions and chives on
top of the chili before
rolling up for a loaded
chili dog.

Preheat oven to 350°F (180°C). Spray
12 regular size muffin cups with
cooking spray.

Unroll crescent rolls and separate along
perforation marks. Cut hot dogs into
1-inch (2.5-cm) pieces and cut horizontally
in half. Place hot dogs flat-side down in
center of dough. Add a spoonful of chili
on top of hot dog and sprinkle with about
a tablespoon (15g) of shredded cheese.
Fold and roll edges of crescent roll over
hot dog and pinch edges closed. Transfer
roll to a muffin cup. Continue to make
rolls and transfer them to tin in same
manner. Bake for 8–10 minutes, until rolls
are golden brown.

Remove tin from oven and, using a knife
or mini metal spatula, transfer chili dog
rolls to plates. Serve with ketchup or
extra chili for dipping.

CHICKEN FAJITAS

MAKES 12 fajitas

PREP TIME: 15 minutes

3 tablespoons (45ml) olive oil
2–3 cups (220g-330g) chicken, cut
    into ½-inch (1.25-cm) cubes
1 cup (120g) red and green bell
    peppers, chopped
1 teaspoon (1.5g) taco seasoning
3 large flour tortillas
1 cup (115g) cheddar cheese, shredded
Optional toppings: sour cream, diced
    tomatoes, cilantro, onion

Preheat oven to 375°F (190°C).

Heat 1 tablespoon (15ml) olive oil in a 10-inch (25.4-cm) skillet over moderate heat until hot but not smoking. Add chicken and peppers and cook, stirring, 5 minutes, or until cooked through. Add taco seasoning and mix well. Remove skillet from heat and set aside.

Spray 12 regular size muffin cups with cooking spray. Put tortillas on a cutting board and cut into fourths. Brush tops with remaining olive oil and tuck each tortilla into a muffin cup, allowing sides to flair up above the cups (see photo). Bake in oven for 5–8 minutes, until edges are nice and golden.

Fill tortilla cups with cooked chicken mixture and top with shredded cheddar cheese. Bake tortillas 3–5 minutes, until cheese is melted.

Remove tin from oven and, with oven mitts, transfer fajitas to plates. Serve immediately with desired toppings.

CHICKEN BURRITO BITES

MAKES 24 bites

PREP TIME: 20 minutes

24 wonton wrappers
2 cups (390g) cooked Mexican rice
1 (16-ounce, 455-g) can black beans,
   drained
1 pound (455g) cooked chicken, diced
½ cup (58g) cheddar cheese, shredded
½ cup (60g) chopped cilantro

TIP:
Leftover diced turkey makes a nice burrito variation.

Preheat oven to 375°F (190°C). Spray 24 regular size muffin cups with cooking spray.

Fit one wonton wrapper into each muffin cup, pressing gently on bottom of tin and allowing sides to fold in gently (see photo). Spray wontons with cooking spray (or brush with melted butter), making sure to cover the edges and tips. Bake wonton cups in oven for 5 minutes, or until brown. Remove tin from oven and set aside.

Mix Mexican rice, black beans, and chicken in a medium bowl. Scoop 1 tablespoon (15g) of mixture into each wonton cup. Top with cheese and bake for 8–10 minutes, until cheese is melted.

Remove bites from oven and sprinkle with chopped cilantro. Using a knife or mini metal spatula, transfer bites to plates. Serve immediately.

SLOPPY JOE CUPS

MAKES 12 sloppy joe cups

PREP TIME: 20 minutes

1 tablespoon (15ml) olive oil
1 pound (455g) ground beef
1 (1.3-oz, 37-g) packet store-bought
  sloppy joe seasoning mix
1 (8-ounce, 225-g) refrigerated
  package Crescent Recipe Creations
  (Seamless Dough Sheet)
3 slices American cheese

Preheat oven to 350°F (180°C). Spray 12 regular size muffin cups with cooking spray.

Heat olive oil in a 10-inch (25.4-cm) skillet over moderate heat until hot but not smoking. Add ground beef and cook, stirring occasionally, about 5 minutes, until browned. Drain meat on a paper towel, discarding any fat in skillet, and return meat to pan. Add sloppy joe seasoning mix and enough water (as indicated on package), and cook according to package directions. Remove skillet from heat and set aside.

While meat cooks: unroll crescent roll sheet and cut into 12 equal squares. Fit one square into each muffin cup, pressing into bottom of cup and up sides.

Spoon sloppy joe mixture into muffin cups, dividing the mixture evenly. Bake for 10 minutes, until heated through.

Cut American cheese slices into fourths and top each muffin cup with one square. Return to oven for 1 minute to melt cheese.

Remove tin from oven and, using a knife or mini metal spatula, transfer sloppy joes to plates. Serve immediately.

BBQ CHICKEN BITES

MAKES 12 bites

PREP TIME: 10 minutes

1 (8-ounce, 255-g) refrigerated
   package Crescent Recipe Creations
   (Seamless Dough Sheet)
2 cups (220g) cooked shredded chicken
2 tablespoons (28ml) bottled BBQ Sauce
1 ½ cups (180g) store-bought coleslaw

Preheat oven to 350°F (180°C). Spray 12 regular size muffin cups with cooking spray.

Unroll crescent roll sheet and cut into 12 squares. Fit one square into each muffin cup.

Mix chicken and BBQ sauce together in a medium bowl and spoon mixture evenly into muffin cups. Bake bites for 12 minutes, until crescent rolls are golden brown.

Remove tin from oven and top bites with coleslaw. Using a knife or mini metal spatula, transfer the bites to plates and serve immediately.

CHEESESTEAK BITES

MAKES 12 bites

PREP TIME 15 minutes

1 ½ tablespoons (25ml) olive oil
1 cup (160g) onion, chopped
1 cup (120g) bell pepper, chopped
Pinch of salt, or to taste
1 (8-ounce, 225-g) refrigerated
  package Crescent Recipe Creations
  (Seamless Dough Sheet)
Pinch of garlic powder, or to taste
8 slices roast beef, chopped
6 slices provolone cheese,
  cut into fourths

Preheat oven to 375°F (190°C). Spray 12 regular size muffin cups with cooking spray.

Heat olive oil in a 10-inch (25.4-cm) skillet over moderate heat until hot but not smoking. Add chopped onion and bell pepper, and cook, stirring, for 5 minutes, until vegetables are softened. Season with a pinch of salt, or to taste.

Unroll crescent roll sheet and cut into 12 squares. Fit one square into each muffin cup. Spoon a heaping tablespoon (15g) of onion mixture into middle of each cup of dough and sprinkle top with a pinch of garlic powder. Divide roast beef among cups and top meat with two pieces of cheese. Bake 8–10 minutes, until cheese is melted.

Remove tin from oven and, using a knife or a mini metal spatula, transfer bites to plates. Serve immediately.

CHEESY CHICKEN BROCCOLI RICE BITES

MAKES 12 bites

PREP TIME: 15 minutes

1 (8-ounce, 225-g) refrigerated
   package Crescent Recipe Creations
   (Seamless Dough Sheet)
2 cups (220g) cooked chicken
1 ½ cups (293g) cooked wild rice,
   prepared according to package
1 ½ cups (107g) steamed broccoli,
   chopped
1 cup (115g) cheddar cheese, shredded

TIP:
For added
creaminess, mix
chickenmixture with
1 cup (252g) cream of
chicken soup.

Preheat oven to 350°F (180°C). Spray
12 regular size muffin cups with
cooking spray.

Unroll crescent roll sheet and cut into
12 squares. Fit one square into each
muffin cup.

Mix chicken, rice, broccoli, and ½ cup
(58g) of cheese in a medium bowl and
spoon into dough cups, dividing it
evenly. Top with remaining cheese. Bake
for 10 minutes, until crescent rolls are
golden brown.

Remove bites from oven. Using a knife
or mini metal spatula, transfer bites to
plates and serve.

MINI SHEPHERD'S PIES

MAKES 12 mini pies

PREP TIME: 20 minutes

1 tablespoon (15ml) olive oil
½ onion, finely chopped
1 pound (455g) ground beef
2 cups (260g) frozen mixed vegetables
    (corn, peas, green beans)
1 ½ tablespoons (25ml) Worcestershire
    sauce
½ cup (120ml) canned beef broth
Salt, to taste
1 (4-ounce, 115-g) package mashed
    potatoes
1 (8-ounce, 225-g) refrigerated
    package Crescent Recipe Creations
    (Seamless Dough Sheet)
1 cup (115g) cheddar cheese, shredded

Preheat oven to 375°F (190°C). Spray 12 regular size muffin cups with cooking spray.

Heat olive oil in a 10-inch (25.4-cm) skillet over moderate heat until hot but not smoking. Add onion and cook, stirring occasionally, for about 3 minutes, until softened. Add the ground beef and cook, stirring occasionally, about 5 minutes, or until meat is cooked through. Drain meat mixture on paper towels and discard fat in skillet. Return meat mixture to pan. Add vegetables, Worcestershire, and beef broth and cook over moderate heat for 10 minutes. Season with salt to taste. Remove skillet from heat and set aside.

Prepare mashed potatoes according to package directions and set aside.

Unroll crescent dough sheet and cut into 12 squares. Fit one square into each muffin cup.

Spoon a heaping tablespoon (15g) of beef mixture into each muffin cup. Sprinkle tops with cheddar cheese, dividing it equally. Spoon one tablespoon (15g) of mashed potatoes on top of each pie and use the back of the spoon to spread evenly over the top. Divide remaining potatoes among tops of the pies, piling it up (this allows the peaks of the potatoes to brown nicely!). Bake 15 minutes, then broil for 5 minutes if the potatoes need browning.

Transfer the tins to a rack and allow the pies to cool for 5 minutes. Using a knife or mini metal spatula, transfer the pies to plates.

TIP:
Skip the crescent rolls and instead use cupcake liners. You'll bake the pies until warmed through, approximately 10 minutes if in liners. (See photo!)

MAC AND CHEESE CUPS

MAKES 12 servings

PREP TIME: 20 minutes

½ pound (225g) elbow macaroni

¼ cup (25g) Parmesan cheese, grated

¼ cup (27g) bread crumbs

1 ½ tablespoons (22g) unsalted butter

2 tablespoons (20g) flour

1 cup (235ml) milk

4 ounces (115g) Gruyère, grated

4 ounces (115g) white cheddar cheese, grated

2 ounces (55g) mild yellow cheddar cheese, grated

2 large egg yolks

Salt to taste

Preheat oven to 425°F (220°C).

Bring a large saucepan of water to a boil. Add the macaroni and cook according to the package directions. Drain the macaroni and set aside.

Combine the Parmesan cheese and bread crumbs in a small bowl. Set aside. Melt the butter in a large saucepan over medium heat. Whisk in the flour and cook the mixture for 2 minutes, whisking constantly. Add the milk and whisk until thick, about 5 minutes. Add the cheeses and whisk until completely melted. Remove pan from the heat and whisk in the egg yolks. Fold in the macaroni and season with salt.

Spray 12 regular size muffin cups with cooking spray. Fill the muffin tins with the macaroni mixture, about three-fourths full. Sprinkle the tops evenly with the bread crumb mixture. Bake 10–12 minutes, until tops are golden.

Remove tin from the oven and transfer to a rack. Let the mac and cheese cool for 5 minutes. Using a knife or mini metal spatula, transfer the cups to plates and serve immediately.

CHICKEN PARMESAN BITES

MAKES 16 bites

PREP TIME: 15 minutes

2 (8-ounce, 225-g) refrigerated
   package Crescent Original
   (8 Dinner Rolls)
1 cup (150g) shredded mozzarella
¾ cup (175ml) bottled marinara sauce
1 small bag frozen popcorn chicken

Preheat oven to 375°F (190°C). Spray 16 regular size muffin cups with cooking spray.

Unroll crescent rolls on a flat surface and separate dough along perforation marks. Place each crescent roll into muffin tin. Put a pinch of mozzarella into center of each roll and spoon 1 tablespoon (15ml) marinara sauce on top. Place one piece of popcorn chicken (two pieces if they are small) on top of sauce. Top chicken with another spoonful of sauce and another pinch of mozzarella. Bake bites in oven for 10–12 minutes, until golden.

Transfer muffin tin to a rack and let bites cool 5 minutes. Using a knife or mini metal spatula transfer bites to a serving plate.

PARTIES & HOLIDAYS

Parties are not a *Reason to Skip the Housework*. When people are coming over, you need to dust and vacuum and get the laundry off the couch. But no matter. Making a roomful of little girls feel like Cinderella or fixing a special treat for special people is totally worth it. Here's the truth: *cooking doesn't have to take all day.* This easy peasy party food can leave guests happy—and you with plenty of energy to enjoy having them there.

CAPRESE BITES

MAKES 12 bites

PREP TIME: 15 minutes

1 (8-ounce, 225-g) package frozen
  pastry dough sheets, thawed
12 small fresh mozzarella balls
6 cherry tomatoes, halved
¼ cup (68g) basil pesto
2 leaves fresh basil (optional)

Set pastry dough sheets out on the counter to thaw. Preheat oven to 375°F (190°C). Spray 12 regular size muffin cups with cooking spray.

Using a 3- to 4-inch (7.5- to 10-cm) glass, cut 12 circles out of pastry sheets and fit into muffin cups. Place a mozzarella ball, cherry tomato half, and a dab of pesto into each cup. Bake 8–10 minutes, or until bubbly and cheese is melted.

Remove tin from oven and transfer to a rack to cool bites for 5 minutes. Using a knife or mini metal spatula, transfer bites to a serving plate. Garnish bites with fresh basil, if desired, and serve warm.

ICE CREAM CUPS

MAKES 12 ice cream scoops

PREP TIME: 5 minutes

12 cupcake liners
1 quart (946ml) ice cream of choice
Optional ingredients: sliced fruit,
    mini chocolate chips, sprinkles,
    mini marshmallows, chopped nuts,
    chocolate sauce, caramel sauce

Place a cupcake liner in each of 12 regular size muffin cups. Scoop one scoop of ice cream into each cupcake liner. Put muffin tin in the freezer until ready to serve.

Before serving, add your favorite toppings.

TIP:
Use a small scoop and arrange several balls of various ice creams for a colorful treat.

BUFFALO CHICKEN CUPS

MAKES 8 chicken cups

PREP TIME: 10 minutes

1 (8-ounce, 225-g) refrigerated
   package Crescent Original
   (8 Dinner Rolls)
1 cup (110g) chopped cooked chicken
1 tablespoon (15ml) Frank's Hot Sauce
¼ cup (120g) diced celery

TIP:
Having a party
and need more?
Use a pound of chicken
and double this recipe
for more bites!

Preheat oven to 375°F (190°C). Spray
8 regular size muffin cups with
cooking spray.

Unroll crescent rolls on a work surface
and separate along perforation marks to
form 8 pieces.

Put remaining ingredients in a bowl and
stir to combine well. Place 1 tablespoon
(15g) of mixture in center of each piece
of dough. Wrap up each piece of dough
by bringing each point to the opposite
side of the dough, making sure that all
mixture is covered. Transfer packages
of dough to the muffin cups and bake
for 12 minutes, or until golden brown.

Remove chicken cups from oven.
Using a knife or mini metal spatula,
transfer the rolls to a serving platter
and serve immediately.

JALAPEÑO POPPER BITES

MAKES 12 mini bites

PREP TIME: 15 minutes

1 (8-ounce, 225-g) refrigerated
package Crescent Recipe Creations
(Seamless Dough Sheet)
2 ounces (55g) cream cheese, cut into
2-inch (5-cm) cubes
1 large jalapeño, diced
3 strips cooked bacon, diced

Preheat oven to 375°F (190°C). Spray 12 mini muffin cups with cooking spray.

Unroll crescent sheet and cut into 12 equal squares. Place each square into muffin tin, pinching any edges that overlap. Place one cream cheese cube into each cup and evenly divide jalapeño and bacon among cups. Bake 8–10 minutes, or until lightly golden.

Transfer muffin tin to a rack and let bites cool 3 minutes. Using a knife or mini metal spatula, transfer bites to a serving plate and serve warm.

TIP:
Use cubed
Velveeta cheese for
a variation on the
original recipe.

DEEP DISH PIZZAS

MAKES 12 pizzas

PREP TIME: 15 minutes

1 (11-oz, 312-g) can refrigerated pizza
crust, (thin crust) or fresh pizza
dough
1 cup (150g) shredded mozzarella
¾ cup (175ml) bottled marinara sauce
½ cup (40g) mini pepperoni
½ cup (55g) cooked Italian sausage
Grated Parmesan cheese, for serving

TIP:
Add vegetables
for a "supreme"
pizza or just use cheese
and marinara sauce
for your pickier
eaters!

Preheat oven to 375°F (190°C). Spray
12 mini muffin cups with cooking spray.

Roll out pizza dough and cut into twelve
2-inch (5-cm) squares. Place one square
into each muffin tin and pinch any
crust that overlaps onto another cup.
Put a pinch of mozzarella into each cup.
Spoon 1 tablespoon (15g) sauce into
each tin. Divide pepperoni and sausage
among cups and sprinkle tops with
remaining mozzarella. Bake pizzas for
13 minutes, until bubbling and golden.

Transfer muffin tin to a rack and let
pizzas cool 5 minutes. Using a knife or
mini metal spatula, remove pizzas from
cups and transfer to a serving plate.
Serve warm sprinkled with Parmesan.

GARLIC BITES

MAKES 8 bites

PREP TIME: 10 minutes

1 (8-ounce, 225-g) refrigerated
   package Crescent Recipe Creations
   (Seamless Dough Sheet)
4 tablespoons (55g) butter, softened,
   or spreadable margarine
1 tablespoon (5g) dried oregano,
   crumbled
1 ½ tablespoons (21g) garlic salt

Preheat oven to 350°F (180°C). Spray 8 mini muffin cups with cooking spray.

Roll out crescent sheet on a work surface and spread with butter to cover the entire sheet. Sprinkle sheet evenly with half the oregano and half the garlic salt. Roll the sheet up, sprinkle with remaining oregano and garlic salt, and cut into 8 even sections. Place each section into a muffin cup and bake for 13–15 minutes, until lightly browned.

Remove tin from the oven. Using a knife or mini metal spatula, transfer the bites to a serving platter. Serve immediately.

TIP:
These are great mini bites for party guests. You might want to make double the recipe so you can refill the plate halfway through the party!

VEGGIE PIZZA BITES

MAKES 8 mini bites

PREP TIME: 20 minutes

1 (8-ounce, 225-g) refrigerated package Crescent Original (8 Dinner Rolls)

1 (8-ounce, 225-g) package cream cheese, softened

½ cup (115g) sour cream

½ package (.5 ounce, 14g) Ranch dressing mix

¼ cup (18g) finely chopped broccoli

¼ cup (38g) finely chopped cauliflower

¼ cup (30g) finely chopped red and green bell peppers

Preheat oven to 350°F (180°C). Spray 8 mini muffin cups with cooking spray.

Unroll crescent rolls on a work surface and separate along perforation marks. Place one piece of dough into each muffin cup. Bake 6–8 minutes until very lightly browned. The cups must be very soft! Remove from oven and set aside.

Mix cream cheese, sour cream, and dressing mix in a small bowl until no lumps remain. Scoop a small amount of dip into each muffin cup. Top with chopped raw veggies.

Using a knife or mini metal spatula, transfer veggie pizzas to a platter and serve immediately.

5 LAYER DIP CUPS

MAKES 12 dip cups

PREP TIME: 20 minutes

3 flour tortillas
1 tablespoon (15ml) olive oil
3 cups (714g) canned refried beans
2 teaspoons (12g) salt
1 cup (115g) cheddar cheese, shredded
Optional toppings: sour cream,
    diced tomatoes, cilantro, onion,
    lettuce, guacamole, salsa, tomatoes

Preheat oven to 350°F (180°C). Spray 12 regular size muffin cups with cooking spray.

Put tortillas on a cutting board and cut each tortilla into fourths. Brush both sides with olive oil. Fit each tortilla into a muffin cup and toast in oven for 5–8 minutes, until edges are nice and golden.

Fill tortilla cups with beans and season with salt. Sprinkle cheddar cheese over tortillas and add optional toppings of your choice in layers.

CRANBERRY BRIE ROLL-UPS

MAKES 8–12 roll-ups
depending on preferred size

PREP TIME: 10 minutes

2 frozen pastry dough sheets, thawed
2 ounces (55g) Brie cheese, softened
1 (14-ounce, 397-g) can cranberry
sauce or whole cranberries

TIP:
Not a fan of Brie?
Try substituting
spreadable
cream cheese.

Put pastry dough sheets on counter and let thaw. Preheat oven to 350°F (180°C). Spray 8–12 regular size muffin cups with cooking spray.

Unroll pastry sheet on a work surface and spread cheese over pastry with a knife, from edge to edge. Spoon cranberry sauce onto top of cheese and spread over cheese (use as much or as little as you like). Roll pastry sheet up and cut into 1-inch (2.5-cm) pieces for small rolls or 2-inch (5-cm) pieces for larger rolls. Place a roll into each muffin cup. Bake 25 minutes, until center of pastry roll is fully cooked.

Using a knife or mini metal spatula, transfer rolls to a platter and serve immediately.

MINI GREEN BEAN CASSEROLES

MAKES 8 mini casseroles

PREP TIME: 15 minutes

1 (15-ounce, 426-g) can refrigerated biscuits

1 (12-ounce, 340-g) can green beans, drained

½ can (5.25 ounces, 149g) cream of mushroom soup

¼ cup (60ml) milk

¼ cup (14g) canned french fried onions

Preheat oven to 375°F. Spray 8 regular size muffin cups with cooking spray.

Roll each biscuit into a ball and press one ball into each muffin cup, pressing the dough up onto the sides. Mix green beans, mushroom soup, and milk in a medium bowl and spoon evenly into muffin tins. Top with french fried onions and bake for 10–12 minutes, until biscuits are golden brown.

Using a knife or mini metal spatula, transfer the mini casseroles to a platter and serve immediately.

TURKEY STUFFING BITES

MAKES 12 bites

PREP TIME: 15 minutes

1 (8-ounce, 225-g) refrigerated
   package Crescent Recipe Creations
   (Seamless Dough Sheet)
1 (6-ounce, 170-g) package instant
   stuffing mix
2 cups (175g) cooked turkey, diced
¼ cup (59g) store-bought turkey gravy

TIP:
Top with a
scoop of cranberry
relish for the perfect
Thanksgiving leftover
meal!

Preheat oven to 350°F (180°C). Spray
12 regular size muffin cups with
cooking spray.

Unroll crescent roll sheet and cut into
12 equal squares. Place a square into
each muffin cup and press down, keeping
the dough pressed against the sides.

Prepare the stuffing according to
package directions. Spoon a tablespoon
(15g) of stuffing into each muffin cup.
Divide diced turkey among cups and
top with ½ tablespoon (7.5g) of gravy.
Bake for 10–12 minutes, until roll is
golden brown.

Remove the tin from the oven and, using
a knife or mini metal spatula, transfer
bites to plates. Serve immediately.

CRISPY TREAT NESTS

MAKES 12 Peep nests

PREP TIME: 10 minutes

¼ cup (55g) butter
1 (10-ounce, 280-g) bag large
  marshmallows
6 cups (72g) Rice Krispies cereal
12 Peeps (marshmallow Easter chicks)

TIP:
Not a fan of Peeps? Fill your nests with jelly beans or M&M's for a fun spring treat!

Melt butter in a large pot over medium heat. Add marshmallows and stir constantly until melted. Remove pot from heat. Add Rice Krispies cereal and stir until well mixed. Fill 12 regular size muffin cups with the mixture and press down in the center with your fingers to make a small indentation for the peep to sit in. Let krispies cups rest in tin 5 minutes to harden slightly.

With a knife or mini metal spatula, remove cups from tin and place one peep on top of each treat.

TWICE-BAKED POTATO CUPS

MAKES 12 cups

PREP TIME: 10 minutes

3 cups (675g) mashed potatoes
(leftovers or store-bought family
size pouch)
1 large egg, lightly beaten
1 cup (115g) shredded cheddar cheese,
divided
3 tablespoons (5g) cooked bacon,
chopped
Fresh chopped chives (optional)
1 cup (230g) sour cream (optional)

Preheat oven to 375°F (190°C). Spray 12 regular size muffin cups with cooking spray.

Stir together the mashed potatoes, egg, ¾ cup (85g) cheddar cheese, and 2 tablespoons (3.5g) chopped bacon. Using an ice cream scoop, divide the potato mixture evenly among the muffin cups, packing the potatoes down into each cup. Bake for 30–35 minutes, until golden brown and crisp around the edges.

Remove tin from the oven, top the potato mixture with the remaining ¼ cup (30g) cheddar cheese, and return to the oven for 3 more minutes.

Remove tin from the oven and transfer to a rack. Let potatoes cool for 5 minutes

Using a knife or mini metal spatula, transfer the potato cups to a serving dish and top with the remaining tablespoon of chopped bacon. Serve immediately.

SWEET TREATS

Dessert in muffin tin–sized servings is way better than a spoon and a carton of ice cream. One can actually feel virtuous having only had a small bite-size piece of heaven. Double score when a recipe only takes minutes to make. That way you don't have to wait long to satisfy a sweet tooth. Better yet, make a batch of treats ahead of time, put the majority in the freezer, and congratulate yourself for showing remarkable restraint.

SNICKERDOODLE ROLLS

MAKES 8 rolls

PREP TIME: 15 minutes

¼ cup (50g) granulated white sugar
1 tablespoon (7.8g) ground cinnamon
About 2 tablespoons (28g) melted
  butter, divided
1 (8-ounce, 225-g) package
  Crescent Rounds
1 cup (100g) confectioners' sugar
½ teaspoon (2.1g) vanilla extract
1 tablespoon (15g) milk

Preheat oven to 350°F (180°C). Spray 8 regular size muffin cups with cooking spray.

Mix sugar and cinnamon in a small shallow bowl. Put melted butter in another shallow bowl. Brush a crescent round with some of the melted butter, then place round in cinnamon mixture and roll around until completely covered on both sides. Place the crescent round into a muffin cup. Coat remaining rounds in same manner, transferring them to muffin cups. Bake 8–10 minutes, until puffed and browned.

Make glaze while cinnamon rounds bake: mix the confectioners' sugar, 1 tablespoon (14g) butter, and the vanilla together in a small bowl. Add half the milk and stir mixture to make a thick glaze, then add more milk, just a drop at a time, until you reach the desired thickness. (You want the glaze to be ideal for drizzling!)

Remove tin from oven and transfer to a cooling rack. Immediately drizzle glaze over rolls and let rolls cool slightly. Using a knife or mini metal spatula, transfer snickerdoodles to a platter. Serve warm or at room temperature.

SUGAR COOKIE FRUIT CUPS

MAKES 12 cookie cups

PREP TIME: 15 minutes

1 (16.5-ounce, 468-g) package refrigerated sugar cookie dough
1 (8-ounce, 225-g) package Cool Whip
1 (8-ounce, 225-g) package cream cheese, softened
Fresh fruit

Preheat oven to 350°F (180°C). Spray 12 mini muffin cups with cooking spray.

Roll cookie dough into twelve 1-inch (2.5-cm) balls. Press one ball into each muffin cup, pressing the dough up onto the sides. Bake 8–10 minutes.

Make the spread while the cookie cups bake: mix together Cool Whip and cream cheese in a small bowl until smooth.

Remove tin from oven and transfer to a rack to let cookie dough cups cool completely. Using a knife or mini metal spatula, transfer cookie cups to a tray. Using a mini cookie dough scooper, scoop spread mixture into cookie cups. Top with fresh fruit!

BANANA CREAM PIES

MAKES 12 pies

PREP TIME: 15 minutes

1 (16.5-ounce, 468-g) package
  refrigerated sugar cookie dough
1 (3.4-ounce, 96-g) box banana
  cream pudding
2 cups (150g) Cool Whip
1 banana (optional)

TIP:
Change up your
pie flavors by using
vanilla pudding,
lemon pudding, or
even chocolate
pudding!

Preheat oven to 350°F (180°C). Spray
12 mini muffin cups with cooking spray.

Roll cookie dough into twelve 1-inch
(2.5-cm) balls. Press one ball into each
muffin cup, pressing the dough up onto
the sides. Bake 8–10 minutes.

While the cookie dough cups bake:
make the banana pudding according
to package directions and chill in
refrigerator.

When cookie cups are baked, remove
tin from oven and transfer to a cooling
rack to cool completely.

Using a mini cookie dough scooper,
scoop the chilled pudding into cookie
cups. Top with a small scoop of Cool
Whip and a banana slice, if desired.

MINI CHERRY PIES

MAKES 12 pies

PREP TIME: 15 minutes

1 (14.1-ounce, 400-g) box refrigerated prepared pie crusts

1 (8-ounce, 225-g) can cherry pie filling

2 cups (150g) Cool Whip

Confectioners' sugar, for dusting

Preheat oven to 425°F (220°C). Spray 12 mini muffin cups with cooking spray.

Unroll pie crusts on a work surface. Using a 3- to 4-inch (7.5- to 10-cm) glass as a cutter, cut out twelve rounds from the dough. Press one round into each muffin cup. Using two spoons, spoon 1–2 tablespoons (17-33g) cherry pie filling into crusts. Bake 14–18 minutes, until bubbly.

Remove tin from oven and transfer to a rack to cool pies completely. Using a knife or mini metal spatula, remove pies from tin and top with Cool Whip and dust with confectioners' sugar.

CHOCOLATE PEANUT ICE CREAM PIES

MAKES 24 pies

PREP TIME: 30 minutes, plus overnight

¾ cup (167g) butter or margarine

2 cups (160g) vanilla wafer crumbs

2 cups (200g) confectioners' sugar

3 large eggs

6 ounces (170g) semisweet chocolate chips, melted

1 ½ cups (216g) salted peanuts, chopped

½ gallon (1.9 litres) vanilla ice cream, softened

Melt ¼ cup (55g) of the butter in a microwave-safe bowl in the microwave. Add vanilla wafer crumbs and stir to combine. Press crumbs into the bottom of 24 regular size muffin cups.

Beat together remaining ½ cup (112g) butter and the confectioners' sugar in a large bowl with an electric mixer until creamy. Beat in eggs, one at a time, then beat in chocolate until well blended. Fold in 1 cup (144g) of the peanuts. Spoon 1–2 tablespoons (15-28g) of mixture into each cup (depending on how thick you want this layer). Transfer muffin tins to freezer for about 30 minutes, until chocolate is firm.

Spoon ice cream into each cup, dividing it evenly, and spread evenly. Sprinkle tops with remaining ½ cup (72g) peanuts. Cover tins with aluminum foil and freeze overnight until firm.

Remove tins from freezer and let pies stand at room temperature 5–10 minutes to soften slightly. Using a knife or mini metal spatula, transfer pies to a plate and serve immediately.

TIP:
You can use your favorite ice cream flavors to change things up! Try a Caramel Chocolate Swirl or Mint Chocolate Chip for new flavors.

MINI PINEAPPLE UPSIDE DOWN CAKES

MAKES 36 cakes

PREP TIME: 15 minutes

⅓ cup (75g) butter, melted
¾ cup (170g) brown sugar
1 (8-ounce, 225-g) can pineapple chunks
1 (10-ounce, 280-g) jar maraschino cherries
1 box yellow cake mix

Preheat oven to 350°F (180°C). Spray 36 mini muffin cups with cooking spray.

Spoon a little less than ½ teaspoon (2.37g) melted butter into each muffin cup. Sprinkle brown sugar into cups (directly into the butter), dividing it evenly among cups. Cut 18 pineapple chunks in half and cut 18 cherries in half. (Reserve any leftover fruit for another use.) Place one piece of pineapple and one piece of cherry in bottom of cup (see photo). Prepare cake mix according to package directions. Spoon cake batter over fruit, filling muffin cups three-fourths full, and bake for 12–15 minutes, until cakes are golden brown.

Remove tins from oven and transfer to a rack to let cakes cool 3 minutes. Working with oven mitts on and dealing with one tin at a time, invert a plate over the tin. Holding the plate and tin together, flip the tin over to release the cakes onto the plate. Serve warm or at room temperature.

BROWNIE PINWHEELS

MAKES 16 rolls

PREP TIME: 10 minutes

1 (18.4-ounce, 522-g) box brownie mix
2 (8-ounce, 225-g) refrigerated
    packages Crescent Recipe Creations
    (Seamless Dough Sheet)
Prepared chocolate sauce (optional)

Preheat oven to 350°F (180°C). Spray 16 regular size muffin cups with cooking spray.

Prepare brownie mix according to package directions. Unroll crescent roll sheets. Using a spatula, spread a very thin later of brownie mix on each crescent roll sheet, making sure to cover the sheets edge to edge. (Note: a very thin layer is important since it takes longer for the brownie mix to cook than it takes to bake the crescent roll!) Roll up each crescent roll sheet and cut each into 8 sections. Place each section into a muffin tin cup and bake for 12–15 minutes, until brownie centers come out clean when tested with a toothpick.

Remove tins from oven and transfer to a rack for 5 minutes, to let pinwheels cool slightly. Using a knife or mini metal spatula, transfer pinwheels to the rack. Drizzle with chocolate sauce or melted chocolate for the perfect treat!

CHOCOLATE PUDDING PIE CUPS

MAKES 12 cups

PREP TIME: 10 minutes, plus 30 minutes chilling time

1 ¼ cup (90g) graham cracker crumbs
⅓ cup (75g) butter, melted
3 tablespoons (38g) sugar
1 (3.5-ounce, 99-g) box chocolate pudding mix
Cool Whip and fresh fruit, for serving (optional)

Spray 12 mini muffin cups with cooking spray.

Mix graham cracker crumbs, butter, and sugar in a medium bowl and press into muffin cups, pressing down and up onto the sides to create bowl shape crusts. Transfer tin to refrigerator and chill crusts for 30 minutes, or bake in a 350°F (180°C) oven for 8 minutes.

Meanwhile, make chocolate pudding according to package directions and refrigerate for 30 minutes.

Spoon chocolate pudding into graham cracker crusts, filling cups three-fourths full. Refrigerate pudding cups for at least 15 minutes before serving.

Using a knife or mini metal spatula, transfer pie cups to a platter. Top with Cool Whip and fresh fruit, if desired.

CINNAMON TORTILLA CUPS

MAKES 8 cups

PREP TIME: 10 minutes

1 teaspoon (4.17g) granulated sugar
½ teaspoon (1.3g) cinnamon
2 tablespoons (28g) butter, melted
2 full size flour tortillas
8 scoops ice cream of choice
Prepared chocolate sauce, for serving
  (optional)

Preheat oven to 350°F (180°C).

Mix sugar and cinnamon in a small bowl and set aside. Brush melted butter onto one side of tortillas. Sprinkle sugar mixture evenly on top and shake off excess. Cut tortillas in fourths and press into 8 regular size muffin cups. Bake for 8–10 minutes, until tortillas are crisp.

Transfer tin to a rack and let tortilla cups cool 5 minutes. Remove cups from tin and fill each with a scoop of ice cream. Drizzle tops with chocolate sauce, if desired, and serve immediately.

CHOCOLATE CHIP COOKIE ICE CREAM BITES

MAKES 12 cups

PREP TIME: 10 minutes

1 (16.5-ounce, 468-g) package refrigerated chocolate chip cookie dough

12 small scoops vanilla ice cream

Prepared chocolate sauce, for serving (optional)

Preheat oven to 375°F (190°C). Spray 12 mini muffin cups with cooking spray.

Roll cookie dough into twelve 1-inch (2.5-cm) balls. Press one ball into each muffin cup, pressing the dough up onto the sides. Bake for 20–24 minutes, until golden brown.

Transfer tin to a rack and let chocolate chip cups cool completely. The center of cups will indent slightly upon cooling, or, if desired, use a 1-inch (2.5-cm) cup and press lightly on center of cookie to make an indentation.

Using a knife or mini metal spatula, remove cookie cups from tin and top with a scoop of ice cream and chocolate sauce, if desired.

COOKING WITH KIDS

Encouraging children to cook is the rage these days. Some of the things young chefs are turning out on TV and in the magazines are pretty amazing. Good for them, but this is what goes on in our kitchen. Sami can stir, shake, sprinkle, and pat down dough with the best of them. She tastes as she goes along, makes a pretty big mess, and has a great time. That works for me. Here are some of the recipes we've collaborated on.

TURKEY CHEDDAR MELTS

MAKES 12 cups

PREP TIME: 10 minutes

3 pita breads, cut in fourths
1 cup (115g) cheddar cheese, shredded
1 cup (175g) turkey sandwich meat, diced

TIP:
Let your little helpers add chopped tomato and lettuce for an even heartier treat!

Preheat oven to 375°F (190°C). Spray 12 regular size muffin cups with cooking spray.

Place a pita bread piece into each muffin cup and spray pita breads with cooking spray (or brush with melted butter), making sure to cover the edges and tips. Bake in oven for 5 minutes, or until brown.

Remove tin from oven. Toss cheddar cheese and turkey in a small bowl until well mixed. Divide turkey-cheese mixture evenly among pita cups and bake in oven 5–8 minutes, until cheese is melted.

Using a knife or small metal spatula, remove turkey-cheddar cups from tins and serve warm.

PIZZA ROLL-UPS

MAKES 8 roll-ups

PREP TIME: 10 minutes

1 (14.1-ounce, 400-g) can refrigerated
    pizza dough (thin crust)
1–2 cups (235-475ml) bottled
    marinara sauce
Dash of dried oregano
Dash of dried basil
2 cups (230g) shredded mozzarella
    cheese
¾ cup (60g) pepperoni slices
1 cup (80g) shredded Parmesan

Preheat oven to 400°F (200°C). Spray
8 regular size muffin cups with
cooking spray.

Unroll refrigerated pizza dough and
top with marinara sauce. Sprinkle on
oregano and basil. Spread shredded
mozzarella cheese and pepperoni evenly
over dough, then spread shredded
Parmesan to cover dough.

Beginning with a long side, roll up
dough jelly-roll fashion and pinch seam
to seal. Cut rolls into 1-inch (2.5-cm)
slices and place a roll, cut side up, into
each muffin cup. Bake 10 minutes, or
until cheese is bubbling.

Using a knife or a mini metal spatula,
transfer the roll-ups to individual plates
and serve immediately.

HAM AND EGG CUPS

MAKES ANY NUMBER of cups

PREP TIME: 10 minutes

Thick slices of cooked ham or turkey
Eggs
Scallions, finely chopped
Salt and freshly ground pepper,
   to taste

Preheat oven to 375°F (190°C). Spray regular size muffin cups, as many as you'll need, with cooking spray.

Place one slice of ham or turkey in bottom of each muffin cup. Crack an egg into the middle of each ham or turkey cup. Sprinkle the tops with scallions and season with salt and pepper. Bake for 20 minutes, or until the eggs are cooked.

TIP:
Let your little helpers put the ham into the cups and crack the eggs into them. Just watch out for shells!

S'MORES POCKETS

MAKES 8 pockets

PREP TIME: 15 minutes

1 (8-ounce, 225-g) refrigerated
   package Crescent Original
   (8 Dinner Rolls)
1 cup (50g) mini marshmallows
2 (1.55-ounce, 44-g) Hershey
   chocolate bars, each broken into
   squares at indents
1 cup (72g) graham cracker crumbs
1 tablespoon (14g) melted butter
1 tablespoon (12.5g) raw sugar

TIP:
Little helpers
will love placing the
marshmallows into
each tin. They'll also be
thrilled to add the
chocolate and brush
the melted butter
on top!

Preheat oven to 350°F (180°C). Spray 8 regular size muffin cups with cooking spray.

Unroll crescent rolls and separate along perforation marks. Put the crescent rolls on a flat surface and divide marshmallows, chocolate, and graham crackers among rolls. Fold over the overhanging edges of the crescent roll so they cover the ingredients and pinch the tops together to form a pocket. Transfer pockets to muffin cups. Brush some melted butter on the top of each pocket and sprinkle with raw sugar. Bake 10–12 minutes, until golden brown.

Using a knife or mini metal spatula, transfer the pockets to a serving plate and serve warm.

PANCAKE BITES

MAKES 12 bites

PREP TIME: 10 minutes

1 cup (122g) store-bought pancake mix
Optional mix-ins: fresh fruit,
   chocolate chips, chopped nuts,
   marshmallows
Pancake syrup for dipping or
   powdered sugar for dusting,
   (optional)

TIP:
Let your little
helpers add their
own toppings to
their pancakes!

Preheat oven to 375°F (190°C). Spray 12 regular size muffin cups with cooking spray.

Prepare pancake batter according to the box instructions in a large bowl. Mix in any toppings you'd like to have in all pancakes. Spoon mixture evenly into muffin cups, filling each three-quarters full. Add any additional toppings, as desired, to individual pancakes. Bake for 8–10 minutes, or until cooked through.

Transfer tin to a rack and let pancakes rest for 5 minutes. Loosen the edges of the pancakes with a knife and, with the knife or a mini metal spatula, transfer the pancakes to plates. Serve warm with syrup for dipping or sprinkle with powdered sugar.

MINI CINNIS

MAKES 12 mini rolls

PREP TIME: 15 minutes

2 teaspoons (8.4g) granulated sugar

1 teaspoon (8.34g) cinnamon

1 (8-ounce, 225-g) refrigerated package Crescent Recipe Creations (Seamless Dough Sheet)

2 tablespoons (28g) butter, melted

⅓ cup (33g) confectioners' sugar

2 teaspoons (10ml) milk

½ teaspoon (2.1ml) vanilla extract

TIP:
Let your little helpers drizzle the rolls with the glaze.

Preheat oven to 350°F (180°C). Spray 12 mini muffin cups with cooking spray.

Mix sugar and cinnamon in a small bowl and set aside.

Unroll crescent roll sheet on a work surface. Brush sheet with melted butter and sprinkle sugar mixture on top. Cut crescent roll sheet into fourths and roll each square up tightly. Cut each roll into three pieces and place one roll in each muffin cup. Bake 8–10 minutes, until rolls are golden brown.

While rolls are baking, mix confectioners' sugar, milk, and vanilla extract in a medium bowl and set aside.

Remove tin from oven and transfer to a rack to let rolls cool for 5 minutes. Using a knife or mini metal spatula, transfer rolls to the rack and drizzle with glaze. Serve warm.

DISAPPEARING MARSHMALLOW PUFFS

MAKES 8 puffs

PREP TIME: 10 minutes

1 (8-ounce, 225-g) refrigerated package Crescent Original (8 Dinner Rolls)

¼ cup (50g) granulated sugar

1 teaspoon (2.6g) cinnamon

8 large marshmallows

2 tablespoons (28g) butter, melted

TIP:
Yes, the marshmallows disappear (melt) into the cinnamon sugar and butter coating—yum!

Preheat oven to 350°F (180°C). Spray 8 regular size muffin cups with cooking spray.

Unroll crescent rolls and separate along perforation marks. Mix sugar and cinnamon in a small bowl. Working with one marshmallow at a time, roll marshmallow in melted butter and then roll in cinnamon-sugar mixture until completely coated. Place the coated marshmallow on a crescent roll, fold in the edges to enclose the marshmallow, and pinch edges together. Transfer the roll to a muffin cup. Make more rolls in same manner and transfer them to the muffin cups. Bake puffs 12–14 minutes, until lightly golden.

Remove tin from oven and, using a knife or mini metal spatula, transfer puffs to a platter. Serve immediately.

HAM AND CHEESE BITES

MAKES 12 bites

PREP TIME: 10 minutes

1 (8-ounce, 225-g) refrigerated
   package Crescent Recipe Creations
   (Seamless Dough Sheet)
2 cups (300g) diced cooked ham
3 slices American cheese (2.25 ounces,
   63g), cut into small squares

Preheat oven to 350°F (180°C). Spray
12 regular size muffin cups with
cooking spray.

Unroll crescent roll sheet and cut into
12 equal squares. Fit one square into
each muffin cup. Divide ham equally
among cups and top with cheese. Bake
for 10–12 minutes, until crescent rolls
are golden brown.

Remove tin from oven and, using a knife
or mini metal spatula, transfer bites to
plates. Serve immediately.

TIP:
Let your little
helpers put the ham
and cheese into
the cups.

BERRY CRESCENTS

MAKES 8 bites

PREP TIME: 10 minutes

½ tablespoon (3.9g) cinnamon
½ tablespoon (6.25g) sugar
1 (8-ounce, 225-g) refrigerated
    package Crescent Original
    (8 Dinner Rolls)
1 cup (110-145g) fresh berries
    (strawberries, blueberries,
    blackberries, and/or raspberries)
Cool Whip or ice cream for serving

TIP:
Let your
little helpers add
the berries to
the rolls.

Preheat oven to 375° F (190°C). Spray 12 regular size muffin cups with cooking spray.

Mix cinnamon and sugar together in a small bowl. Unroll crescent rolls and separate along perforation marks. Put the crescent rolls on a flat surface and sprinkle rolls with cinnamon mixture. Divide berries evenly among rolls. Bring long end of dough up to the top of the triangle, and bring each corner in to the center to form a small pocket. It's ok to have a few open spots! Transfer each crescent to a muffin cup. Bake 8–10 minutes, until golden brown.

Remove the tin from the oven and transfer to a rack. Let the rolls cool for 3–5 minutes. Using a knife or small metal spatula, transfer the rolls to bowls and serve immediately with Cool Whip or ice cream.

HEALTHIER OPTIONS

The other day our five-year-old actually chose edamame instead of a Popsicle. Mom score! This is proof that "healthier" options aren't yucky. If you like the portion control and ease of muffin tin meals, it's an easy step to work in whatever nutritional goals you have. To get started, here are some of the recipes that I make. They're simple, delicious, and nutritious.

SPINACH EGG FRITTATAS

MAKES 12 frittata cups

PREP TIME: 10 minutes

⅓ cup (55g) packaged pre-cooked
   turkey sausage (optional)
½ cup (15g) chopped spinach
⅓ cup (74g) finely chopped zucchini
¼ cup (20g) Parmesan cheese, shredded
6 large eggs
1 large tomato, chopped
Green tops of 2 scallions, chopped

Preheat oven to 350°F (180°C). Spray 12 regular size muffin cups with cooking spray.

Mix together sausage (if using), spinach, zucchini, and cheese in a medium bowl. Crack eggs into a medium bowl, add 1 tablespoon (15ml) water, and whisk together. Add eggs to the spinach mixture and, using a fork, mix all ingredients together. Divide frittata mixture evenly among muffin cups and bake for 15 minutes, or until eggs are firm.

Remove tin from oven. Using a knife or mini metal spatula, cut around edges of tin cups and transfer frittata cups to plates to serve. Top with tomato pieces and scallion greens and serve immediately.

QUINOA EGG BURRITOS

MAKES 8 mini burritos

PREP TIME: 15 minutes

2 (6-inch, 15-cm) soft whole wheat
   tortillas
6 large eggs
1 cup (46g) cooked quinoa
⅓ cup (55g) packaged pre-cooked
   ground turkey sausage
¼ cup (30g) shredded cheddar cheese
Bottled salsa as an accompaniment
   (optional)

Preheat oven to 350°F (180°C). Spray
8 regular size muffin cups with
cooking spray.

Cut tortillas into fourths and place one
tortilla piece into each muffin cup.

Crack eggs into a medium bowl, add
1 tablespoon (15ml) water, and whisk
together. Add cooked quinoa and
sausage to egg mixture and stir to
combine.

Spray a medium skillet with cooking
spray. Heat skillet over medium-high
heat until hot but not smoking. Pour
egg mixture into hot skillet, and, using
a rubber spatula, stir the eggs as they
scramble. Cook eggs until soft.

Divide scrambled egg mixture evenly
among tortilla cups and top with
shredded cheese. Bake for 5–8 minutes,
until cheese is melted and eggs are
cooked through.

Remove tin from oven. Fold tortilla
edges in over eggs to form packets and
secure with a toothpick for 5 minutes.
Remove toothpicks and, using a knife
or metal mini spatula, transfer burrito
bites to plates. Serve immediately.

QUINOA SHRIMP SALAD

MAKES 8 salad cups

PREP TIME: 15 minutes

2 soft spinach tortillas or regular
   whole wheat tortillas (10 inch, 25cm)
2 cups (370g) cooked quinoa
1 cup (172g) canned black beans,
   rinsed and drained
1 cup (225g) frozen salad shrimp
¾ cup (38g) cherry tomatoes, cut in half
¼ cup (15g) cilantro
1 avocado
3 tablespoons (45ml) orange juice
2 tablespoons (28ml) olive oil, plus
   additional for brushing tortillas
⅛ teaspoon (.23g) cayenne pepper, or
   to taste
⅛ teaspoon (.75g) salt

Preheat oven to 350°F (180°C).

Cut tortillas into fourths and place one piece into each muffin cup. Spray or brush tortilla cups with olive oil and bake for 5 minutes, until crispy.

Remove tortilla cups from oven and let cool on a rack for 3 minutes.

While tortilla cups cool, make the salad: Combine the quinoa, black beans, shrimp, tomatoes, and cilantro in a large bowl and toss gently to combine. Peel and chop the avocado and add it to the mixture, tossing gently. Whisk together orange juice, 2 tablespoons (28ml) olive oil, cayenne pepper, and salt in a small bowl and set aside.

Using a knife or mini metal spatula, transfer tortilla cups to plates and divide salad among cups. Drizzle orange dressing over salad and serve immediately (you don't want the avocado to brown!).

CHEESY MUSHROOM ASPARAGUS BITES

MAKES 12 bites

PREP TIME: 10 minutes

12 wonton wrappers
Olive oil for brushing wonton
  wrappers
1 ½ cups (120g) Asiago cheese,
  shredded
¼ cup (20g) Parmesan cheese,
  shredded
1 cup (134g) finely chopped asparagus
1 cup (70g) finely chopped mushrooms

Preheat oven to 350°F (180°C). Spray 12 regular size muffin cups with cooking spray.

Fit one wonton wrapper into each muffin cup. Brush top of wrappers with olive oil, especially the tips, and bake in oven for 5 minutes, until lightly golden.

Mix shredded cheeses together in a bowl and set aside.

Remove wonton cups from oven and sprinkle half of the shredded cheese mix into bottom of wonton cups, dividing it evenly. Add a layer of asparagus and mushrooms and top with remaining shredded cheese mix. Bake for 10–12 minutes, until cheese is melted.

Remove tin from oven and, using a knife or metal mini spatula, transfer the bites to a platter. Serve immediately.

SMOOTHIE CUPS

MAKES 6 frozen smoothie cups for 3 smoothies

PREP TIME: 10 minutes

½ cup (120ml) juice, such as orange or apple juice (or coconut water), plus additional ⅓ cup (80ml) juice or coconut water to make each smoothie from the frozen cups
1 cup (20g) spinach
1 banana
½ cup (73g) fresh blueberries
½ cup (65g) frozen fruit

Pour ½ cup (120ml) juice into blender, then add spinach and all fruit. Blend until smooth. Spoon smoothie mixture into 6 regular size muffin cups (preferably using a silicone muffin pan), filling the cups. Place the pan (or tin) in the freezer and let the smoothie cups freeze overnight.

Pop out each smoothie cup if using a silicone muffin pan (if using a normal muffin tin, simply place the tin in a small amount of warm water for a minute to release the cups) and store cups in a freezer bag for up to 2 weeks. Whenever you're ready for a smoothie, add two of the frozen cups to your blender with ⅓ cup (80ml) juice or coconut water and blend until smooth.

FROZEN YOGURT BITES

MAKES 24 mini bites

PREP TIME: 10 minutes

6 ounces (170g) vanilla Greek yogurt
½ cup (30g) light Cool Whip
¾ cup (150g) granola
¼ cup (37g) fresh berries

Mix Greek yogurt and Cool Whip in a medium bowl. Add granola and berries and mix with a spoon. Spoon mixture into mini muffin cups, dividing it evenly, cover with aluminum foil, and freeze at least 6 hours.

Using a knife or mini metal spatula, pop bites out of tin and store in an air-tight container in the freezer.

TIP:
For an added sweet touch, dip in melted chocolate!

PITA CUPS WITH HUMMUS

MAKES 12 cups

PREP TIME: 15 minutes

3 pita breads
1 tablespoon (15ml) olive oil
2 cups (492g) store-bought hummus
½ cup (75g) feta cheese, for garnish

Preheat oven to 375°F (190°C).

Cut each pita bread into fourths. Open up each bread section and fit into 12 regular size muffin cups. Spray or brush pita bread with olive oil, especially the tips. Bake the bread cups in the oven for 8–10 minutes, until the bread is toasted.

Remove muffin tin from oven and spoon hummus into muffin cups, dividing it equally. Sprinkle feta cheese over the hummus. Serve warm or at room temperature!

INDEX

CONVERSIONS

Liquids, Herbs, and Spices

1 teaspoon	=	5 ml
1 tablespoon or ½ fluid ounce	=	15 ml
⅛ cup or 1 fluid ounce	=	30 ml
¼ cup or 2 fluid ounces	=	60 ml
⅓ cup	=	80 ml
½ cup or 4 fluid ounces	=	120 ml
⅔ cup	=	160 ml
¾ cup or 6 fluid ounces	=	180 ml
1 cup or 8 fluid ounces or ½ pint	=	250 ml
1 ½ cups or 12 fluid ounces	=	350 ml
2 cups or 16 fluid ounces or 1 pint	=	500 ml
3 cups or 1 ½ pints	=	700 ml
4 cups or 1 quart or 2 pints	=	1 L
4 quarts or 1 gallon	=	4 L

Weight*

1 ounce	=	28 g
¼ pound or 4 ounces	=	113 g
⅓ pound	=	150 g
½ pound or 8 ounces	=	230 g
⅔ pound	=	300 g
¾ pound or 12 ounces	=	340 g
1 pound or 16 ounces	=	450 g
2 pounds	=	900 g

Note: these conversions do not apply to fluid ounces

Weights of Common Ingredients

All-purpose flour:	1 cup	=	120 g
Granulated cane sugar:	1 cup	=	200 g
Confectioners' sugar:	1 cup	=	100 g
Brown sugar (packed):	1 cup	=	180 g
Cornmeal:	1 cup	=	160 g
Cornstarch:	1 cup	=	120 g
Rice (uncooked):	1 cup	=	190 g
Macaroni (uncooked):	1 cup	=	140 g
Oats (uncooked):	1 cup	=	90 g
Butter:	1 cup or 2 sticks	=	240 g
Fruits & vegetables (chopped):	1 cup	=	150 g
Nuts (chopped):	1 cup	=	150 g
Nuts (ground):	1 cup	=	120 g
Bread crumbs (dry):	1 cup	=	150 g
Cheese (shredded):	1 cup	=	115 g
Parmesan cheese (grated):	1 cup	=	90 g

Length

¼ inch	=	6 mm
½ inch	=	13 mm
1 inch	=	2.5 cm

Temperature

°F	°C	°F	°C
250	120	375	190
275	140	400	200
300	150	425	220
325	175	450	230
350	180	475	245